Original title:
Aliens Ate My Homework (and Other Poems)

Copyright © 2025 Creative Arts Management OÜ
All rights reserved.

Author: Dorian Ashford
ISBN HARDBACK: 978-1-80567-783-3
ISBN PAPERBACK: 978-1-80567-904-2

Abductions and Algebra

In the night sky, I saw a ship,
It zapped my math with a little blip.
Numbers twirled in a cosmic dance,
Now my grades are just a chance!

My teacher frowned, she shook her head,
'Your homework's missing!' she loudly said.
I laughed and said, 'In space it flew,
With Martians who wanted to learn too!'

Unsolved Mysteries of Mathematics

X never showed, it ran away,
Left me puzzled in disarray.
Why did seven take a hike?
With eight, they formed an odd strike!

Pi rolled off, it ran amok,
Decimals fled, they formed a flock.
Who thought math could be a game?
I think it's those aliens to blame!

The Homework Saga and the Stars

My essay vanished among the stars,
Rumor is, it's on Mars with cars.
Creatures giggle at my plight,
While I chase down asteroids at night.

I made a list of every task,
But the stardust made me lose track.
Now my notes are in orbit, it seems,
Caught up in intergalactic dreams!

Celestial Calculation Catastrophes

Calculators launched to the sky,
Battling comets as they fly.
With each 'beep', they seemed to cheer,
Until they vanished, oh dear!

Equations tangled like space vines,
Across the cosmos, they draw lines.
Next time I'll tie my homework tight,
So it won't sneak off in the night!

Galaxy's Graded Glitches

In a galaxy far away,
The grades just flew astray.
Papers floating, oh what fun,
Look, there goes another one!

Teachers sigh and scratch their heads,
As homework dances like it's thread.
Stars giggle in the cosmic breeze,
While I just beg for some good grades, please!

Stars Steal My Essays

Twinkling lights with cheeky grins,
Swipe my essays, full of sins.
While I dream of grades so high,
Those stars just wink and fly on by.

I write, I scribble, plot my tale,
Yet cosmic thieves just laugh and wail.
Each line I crafted, poof—it's gone,
Starlit laughter till the break of dawn.

The Day My Report Went Missing

One morning bright, my report's not there,
The dog's asleep, it's not his affair.
I search the nooks, I check the cranny,
Is that a spaceship, oh so uncanny?

My teacher frowns, she needs it now,
I wonder if the stars will take a bow.
I scribble fast, a brand new scene,
While Martians giggle, you know what I mean!

Unseen Invaders

Unseen fiends with sticky hands,
Swiped my projects, made their plans.
While I struggle, they have their fun,
In this cosmic game, I'm clearly done.

Under my bed, they hide with glee,
I can almost hear their strange decree.
"Homework's ours," they chant and cheer,
While I just sit, consumed by fear!

Unfinished Tasks

Tasks unending, piled up high,
Will little critters wave goodbye?
They snicker, they chortle, oh what a sight,
As I toil away by my desk at night.

Each thought I pen, they steal with ease,
Laughing softly 'neath the stars and trees.
It's a cosmic race, it's truly a blast,
With homework vanished, I can't finish fast!

Remarkable Returns from Outer Space

A spaceship landed with a bang,
My math was tossed, my grades all sang.
They borrowed pens, they took my snack,
But left behind a purple pack.

With shiny eyes and silly hats,
They danced around like giggling cats.
They promised to return someday,
To teach me their wacky alien way.

Homework Alienation

My math was due, my notes were bare,
I searched for help, I found a chair.
An alien popped up, quite a sight,
With three big eyes and legs so light.

It scribbled my answers, but oh dear,
The 5's looked like 6's, I shed a tear.
It gave a laugh, and spun away,
Disappearing, but left me to pay.

Cosmic Comet Confusion

A comet zoomed with plenty of flair,
Dropping books like confetti in the air.
I grabbed a few, to my surprise,
They taught me dance moves and funny lies.

I giggled, twirled, then missed the bus,
Now late for school, it caused a fuss.
But who could blame a comet so grand,
For turning homework into a dance band?

The Myth of the Dollar-Store Alien

I bought a toy, a green, little champ,
Thought, 'Is this real? Or just a stamp?'
It blinked and grinned, then started to sing,
I just wanted it to do my math thing.

With glittery shoes and a plastic beam,
It lost me in a very deep dream.
But when I woke up, it didn't stay,
Guess that's how aliens like to play!

Stolen Scribbles from Star Systems

In the night sky, they looked down,
With eyes so big, they stole my crown.
My papers danced on cosmic winds,
They giggled and twirled, oh where to begin?

Math problems flipped like saucers in flight,
As aliens laughed, oh what a sight!
They scribbled notes in neon ink,
I wondered if they could even think!

Cosmic Conspiracy to Dismiss Studies

Was it Pluto or a comet's tail?
Why is my project now a space whale?
They plotted schemes with their silly grins,
To pull my grades down to Jupiter's bins.

"Earthlings study? Not our concern!"
With popcorn snacks, they took their turn.
My essays vanished without a trace,
While space jesters giggled in their place!

Galactic Gabbering on Grade Day

On grade day morn, the news was loud,
Extraterrestrials formed a crowd.
They turned in homework with Crayola hues,
While I stood by, utterly confused.

"Your math's all wrong, but what's our score?"
They shrugged and chuckled, "What's one more?"
Their laughter echoed through the hall,
I fretted about my very small fall.

Rogue Homework and Ridiculous Realities

Homework vanished in a flash,
Was that a meteor? Or merely a splash?
I chased my notes through cosmic streams,
Where nothing was real, just wacky dreams.

"Defy the laws!" the aliens cried,
My study guide had taken a ride.
In a galaxy where grades don't matter,
I learned to laugh and just chatter!

Galactic Gaffes in Grading

My paper flew past Mars,
With scribbles from the stars.
The teacher found it strange,
But thought it was a range.

Extraterrestrial marks,
Left by nibbling sparks.
A comet swung around,
With questions that astound.

I laughed at what I wrote,
In colors that could float.
The grades made quite a mess,
Can I retake this test?

The aliens made notes,
In cosmic, gooey quotes.
I submitted with a grin,
Hoping for a win!

Homework Shock and Awe

Last night my book took flight,
In the glare of the twilight.
Math problems felt so light,
While eating snacks in spite.

The dog and I conspired,
To see what transpired.
A spaceship zoomed on by,
With pizza in the sky!

I wrote a fun report,
On how to play with sport.
But instead of a grade,
A snack was what I made!

So now it's time to chill,
Forget that homework thrill.
With laughter and some cheers,
We'll munch on nachos here!

Stars, Strangers, and Study Sessions

In the quiet of the night,
I met a strange delight.
With stars that winked and danced,
I thought my brain was pranced.

Homework felt like a game,
With aliens to blame.
They asked me of my world,\nAs my pencil twirled.

Each answer brought a cheer,
From creatures far and near.
Their insight was quite neat,
But I missed lunch and meat!

I scribbled silly things,
Like how a planet sings.
When the bell finally rang,
My head with laughter sang!

Space-Time Homework Loops

A wormhole in my room,
Brought knowledge in a bloom.
Curved through cosmic edges,
I wrote in secret pledges.

I solved a riddle bold,
With answers that I sold.
But time whirled back again,
To try that math again.

Continuous detours,
Brought intergalactic scores.
Each attempt led me wild,
Like testing a newborn child.

With every loop I took,
My homework was a book.
Yet laughter filled the void,
No boredom was enjoyed!

When the Universe Interrupted My Studies

My math book flew out the window,
Chased by a spaceship, don't you know.
With calculus lost in a cosmic chase,
I laughed as I watched it drift into space.

The science fair models danced in flight,
Bouncing off planets, oh what a sight!
My pencils twirled in zero gravity,
Creating art that defied sanity.

Homework vanished, replaced by stars,
While aliens jammed on my guitars.
They strummed along to my absent notes,
As I sat perplexed, imagining goats.

With every equation, I'd laughed and cried,
In this cosmic mess, I took it in stride.
Thus the universe showed me one thing,
Never do homework when comets can sing.

Homework Hitches and Celestial Glitches

In the night, my paper took flight,
It zoomed through the air, oh what a sight!
With a whoosh and a whirl, it spun away,
Leaving me stumped on what to say.

The dog barked loud at a glowing light,
As my homework danced like a kite in flight.
Pencil marks shimmered in moonbeam glows,
While I chased down my pets and their bizarre foes.

Had aliens snagged my creative whim?
Or just a giggle from the cosmic brim?
With every page that floated past,
I couldn't help but giggle, this might last!

Papers crumpled like silly string,
In the space chaos, what joy could bring?
Though grades may suffer in cosmic zones,
At least my laughter rolled in happy tones.

Paranormal Pencils and Paper Planets

Pencils were buzzing with crazy zeal,
Sketching galaxies—what a surreal deal!
On paper planets, ideas went wild,
As I giggled like a five-year-old child.

My homework erupted, an interstellar mess,
With wormholes swirling, I must confess.
Each equation became a comet's tail,
As I penned down notes both funny and pale.

Ghostly erasers danced on the desk,
Making funny faces, oh what a fest!
They'd ghost-write my essays, spelling quite wrong,
But somehow, it all felt like I belonged.

While I wielded crayons like lightsabers bright,
Drawing out planets in random delight,
This homework hiccup brought cosmic cheer,
In the end, I laughed loud, with no fear.

The Extraterrestrial Turn-In

I flipped through pages, a cosmic delight,
Waiting for beings to pick up tonight.
They promised to take my homework away,
I chuckled—could they really save the day?

The spaceship hovered, my grades in tow,
With colors that shimmered, all aglow.
They handed me back a bonus surprise,
An A+ sticker that beamed in the skies.

But as they departed, they left quite a mess,
My math book curled up, refusing to guess.
"Send it back," I hollered in glee,
Their navigation failed—oh, poor ET!

So here stood I with a grin and some flair,
An alien crew with homework to spare.
I waved goodbye with a wink and a grin,
Thanking the stars for this funny spin!

Starship Syntax Errors

My essay shot past Pluto,
Like a comet on the run.
Space grammar made it dizzy,
And now it's lost, what fun!

The words were in a jumble,
Floating like a lost balloon.
My teacher called for liftoff,
But it crashed in cosmic June.

Sentences on a rocket,
Zooming through the wasted space.
Drafts re-entering the atmosphere,
With zero chance of grace.

So if you see my homework,
Please send it back to me.
It took a ride on spaceship,
And now it's gone, you see!

The Alien Aversion of Assignment Anxiety

Last night I heard a tapping,
On my window, oh so bright.
An awkward being scratching,
With my homework in its flight.

It had three eyes and tentacles,
Trying hard to read my notes.
While I found it quite comical,
I'm failing, as it floats!

I asked it for my paper,
It just giggled and went flat.
Said it wasn't in its wheelhouse,
It was busy chasing cats!

So here I am in trouble,
Waiting for my grade to drop.
Blame it on the cosmic life,
That made my homework hop!

Scribbles Lost in Space

Orbiting around my desk,
Are scribbles that can't be found.
They've tucked themselves in stardust,
Where no pen can make a sound.

I wrote a poem about Mars,
But now it's floating free.
A black hole took my maths test,
And my science seems to flee!

Each paper seems to giggle,
As they swirl in zero G.
Homework parties in the cosmos,
Why won't they come back to me?

With laughter in the void,
And planets made of cheese,
I chase my lost assignments,
On cosmic, endless knees!

Cosmic Curiosities and Classroom Chaos

The classroom turned to stardust,
When my project hit the wall.
Planets spinning round my mind,
Ideas floating, do they fall?

Markers turned to meteors,
Textbooks, comets lost in flight.
Trying to make sense of chaos,
With an alien's delight.

Homework's now a mystery,
In galaxies unknown.
While teachers ponder orbiting,
My brain feels like a stone.

So when you see my folder,
Shrug and send it on its way.
It's off to Mars for answers,
In a cosmic game we play!

The Interplanetary Homework Dilemma

In a galaxy far away, they play,
With papers that shimmer and sway.
My math was a meal, oh what a steal,
But it vanished! What can I say?

Stardust spilled on my desk, oh dear,
Their laughter echoed, loud and clear.
They munched on my plans, like candy, it seems,
Now my grades are hidden in atmosphere!

Extraterrestrial Excuses

The dog ate my work, I'd often claim,
But now it's from space, that's their game.
With comets so quick, no paper to pick,
My excuse is now cosmic fame.

They say, 'Sorry, we thought it was gold!'
Their cosmic munching, pure stories untold.
Now teachers just frown, my grades tumble down,
While I spin tales of wonders so bold!

Cosmic Crumbs on My Desk

Tiny flakes of starlight, crumbs all around,
My homework a feast, lost without sound.
I sift through the mess, oh what a distress,
With glee, they devoured my thoughts unbound.

Green hands reach up, with giggles they share,
Nibbling on essays, oh life's unfair!
I scribble on napkins, 'cause I have to fight,
To reclaim what is mine from their interstellar snare.

The Day My Essay Vanished

One morning I woke, excitement was high,
My masterpiece ready to impress the sky.
But soon it was gone, like a sneeze on the breeze,
Did they zap it to space without a goodbye?

With laughter in waves and a twinkle in sight,
They beamed up my words, oh what a delight!
I stood there in shock, while they danced on the block,
As my teacher just sighed, 'What a curious plight!'

The Unfortunate Fate of the Unfinished Report

My paper was stunning, a sight to behold,
But aliens swooped in, or so I am told.
They snatched it away, what a terrible blow,
Left me with nothing, just this dreadful woe.

I searched through the cosmos, my work was so bright,
But all that I found was an alien's bite.
They munched on my margins, devoured my lines,
Now I'm left with excuses and silly punchlines.

In hopes for redemption, I typed with great speed,
But they zapped my new draft, oh what a misdeed!
With laughter they zoomed away in their craft,
Leaving me wondering if this is all a laugh.

So here's my confession, in ink stained and smudged,
That aliens, indeed, have truly begrudged.
My homework's in orbit, on a journey so far,
While I'm stuck at my desk, beneath a lone star.

Cosmic Confusion in the Classroom

The teacher was fuming, had lost all her cool,
When I claimed my assignment was lost on a spool.
She blinked in disbelief, as I told my tall tale,
Of creatures on planets who thrive to derail.

They bubble and giggle, these interstellar folks,
They giggle at teachers, and make silly jokes.
With pop quizzes floating on meteoric winds,
Confusing the students, their cosmic chagrins.

My classmates were chuckling, all caught in my ruse,
Of math problems floating, and spelling in blues.
While Venusian kids danced with zeroes and ones,
In this humorous quandary, we all shared the fun.

So here's to confusion, both earthly and grand,
With giggles and chuckles, we stick to the plan.
For homework's a cosmic mischief at best,
Just wait until next time, we'll all be blessed!

Out of This World: Educational Distortions

In a galaxy distant, where structures are strange,
I found my assignments had shifted and changed.
With equations that danced on the beams of a light,
I laughed as I watched paper take flight.

The rulers were rulers of planets unknown,
While erasers were squeezing the seams of my phone.
Each calculation a burst of pure spark,
Whispered secrets of math in the back of the dark.

But learning was swirling, just like in a whirl,
Where physics and poetry twisted and twirled.
My essays became creatures with wings made of ink,
In a universe where homework would not let me think.

So I scribbled and giggled amidst all the lore,
As knowledge became something I could not ignore.
I'll dance with these lessons, so bizarre yet so bright,
In a cosmos of learning that feels just right!

Galactic Graders and Missing Marks

My homework was lost, it flew past the stars,
Grading is tricky on a planet of jars.
With creatures who scribble in colors so bold,
I wondered if grades were just bought and sold.

The graders were squiggles, all zany and free,
They puzzled all answers, just like a bad spree.
With thumbs up for yes, and sideways for no,
Each mark was a mystery that put on a show.

With laughter and joy, I watched them collide,
In cosmic confusion, where no one can hide.
As humor was graded, and mishaps were bright,
Turning my blunders into sheer delight.

So here's to the ruckus that makes grades a game,
In an intergalactic classroom, never the same.
Where cosmic graders giggle at each little quirk,
And homework's just fuel for a kindle of smirk.

Homework Hijacked by Space Dwellers

Late at night, my desk sat bare,
Papers vanished into thin air.
A spaceship landed with a beep,
Now math's with creatures from the deep!

They giggled loud, their voices squeaked,
Challenged me to peek-a-boo peeked.
In zero gravity, we drew a line,
While munching cookies shaped like shine!

My essay?! No, it's their new toy!
They danced around, my paper's joy.
Funky fonts and colors bright,
Homework's lost to cosmic flight!

So if your work has gone away,
Check the stars or ask the sway.
For space dwellers might just delight,
In using homework for their flight!

Celestial Cheaters

In class we shared our glances sly,
While saucer-shaped snacks flew by.
Aliens winked, so full of charm,
Over math, they meant us no harm.

They whispered answers, soft and low,
While trying hard not to let go.
Geometry done with cosmic flair,
Our teacher clueless, unaware!

Gravity jokes flew faster than light,
With jokes and giggles, we took flight.
Tests completed in a cosmic dance,
A humorous spacey academic chance!

While humans fret about their grades,
They just laugh, forget their charades.
Celestial cheaters, oh what a scene,
Turning quizzes into a comedy routine!

Abduction of the Assignment

My report went missing at suppertime,
Stolen away in an alien crime!
Bright eyes stared with laughter loud,
Taking my grades, making me proud!

They flipped through facts like magic tricks,
Dancing around in cosmic kicks.
Homework's now an interstellar quest,
With alien friends, it's the very best!

Diagrams drawn in stardust glow,
Math equations now a joyful show.
They added sparkles to every page,
Turning deadlines into a cosmic stage!

So if your essays fly away,
Just laugh it off and let them play.
Assignments may just find new friends,
In the galaxy where fun never ends!

Martian Mishaps in Academia

In the schoolyard, I heard a beep,
Martians landing in a leap!
With backpacks full of gooey snacks,
They joined our class, no looking back!

They'd mispronounce every tough word,
In rhymes and giggles, laughter stirred.
Their quiz notes faded in thin air,
Creating chaos with wild flair!

Potato science turned to fun,
With alien gadgets, they'd outrun.
No grades to stress, just silly games,
In every mischief, laughter reigns!

So if you see green folks nearby,
Join the fun and let out a sigh.
For Martian mishaps are full of cheer,
Turning school days into laughter here!

Cosmic Curriculum Confusion

In class, we studied stars, oh so bright,
But my paper took a galactic flight.
A spaceship zoomed down with a whoosh,
My facts became fuel for a cosmic swoosh.

Math turned to math with a twist of fate,
Interstellar numbers I just can't translate.
They counted in shapes, I counted in sighs,
As comets laughed, oh how they did rise!

History lessons spun in a whirl,
With Martians debating who gave Earth a twirl.
My notebook became a map to the stars,
Filled with doodles of spaceships and bars.

Next time I study, I must take a chance,
To keep my homework safe from a dance.
Or maybe a lock? Oh, where's my key?
Cosmic chaos, just let me be free!

The Intergalactic Mess

My desk was a portal, swirling with fun,
Homework all tangled, and then it was done.
Spaceships soared in while I took a break,
Math problems vanished; my brain was at stake!

A cosmic ruckus, a chaotically bright,
Comets threw papers like a meteor fight.
They giggled at grammar, and laughed at my pen,
I sighed, "Not again, please leave me, amen!"

Science turned messy, reactions went wild,
As aliens juggled my notes like a child.
In a burst of laughter and candy-floss spritz,
My project transformed into sweets—what a twist!

The teacher showed up, saw the mess, oh dear,
Said, "Are those space snacks or homework I fear?"
With giggles and grins, I acted aloof,
"Just a learning experience—a little goof!"

Homework Hijacked by Spacefarers

Late at night, I heard a strange noise,
A whirling of gadgets, a chorus of joys.
My homework was ready for takeoff, it seemed,
As spacefarers laughed—was I being dreamed?

They bounced on my bed, in helmets so bright,
Swapping my essays for snacks in the night.
I tried to explain that it was all mine,
But they patted my head, said, "This stuff is divine!"

With twinkling green eyes, they boasted a score,
That math from the stars would open new doors.
But wouldn't you know, my writing was lost,
In the whirl of their laughter, it came at a cost!

While I cleaned my room, they zipped out with glee,
My papers had vanished, oh what a spree!
Next time I'll guard all my work with great care,
Maybe keep a spaceship right under my chair!

Extraterrestrial Excuses

When the teacher asked where my work had gone,
I simply replied, "A trip to the dawn!
My homework is orbiting Mars, I believe,
It's on a wild journey, you just can't conceive."

With a wink and a grin, I bought a little time,
'Cause the truth of my tale had turned into rhyme.
Those creatures from space took my paper for fun,
To prove math is better when it's under a sun!

In class they returned, stars twinkling in sight,
My project was shiny, a pure cosmic light.
"Look!" they all cheered, "What a grand piece of art!"
While I just sat chuckling, my grin wouldn't part.

The bell rang, I knew I'd make it through,
With my cosmic excuse, oh, what else could I do?
For when homework went wild in a wondrous delight,
I learned that the universe is humor—so bright!

Night Sky Inspirations and Homework Frustrations

Stars twinkle bright, in my room so small,
A math book that screams, "Do your homework, y'all!"
I glance out the window, the cosmos at play,
While fractions and decimals lead me astray.

My cat steals my pencil; what a silly scene,
Plans for a spaceship turn into a meme.
The universe dances, I'm lost in its glow,
But papers and projects are stealing the show.

In the dark I can hear all the planets collide,
But my teacher just wants me to get my work tied.
I scribble some doodles of astronauts blue,
Wishing my homework would just vanish too!

With laughter and giggles, I summon my fate,
Homework's a monster I cannot quite sate.
Time's slipping away in the celestial rush,
In the night sky, my thoughts make a splash!

Beyond the Homework Horizon

Beyond the horizon where bright comets zoom,
Lies a planet of dragons who help with the gloom.
"Let's skip the math test!" they holler and shout,
And blast through the sky with a cosmic clout.

They scribble equations with tails of pure flame,
While I sit and chuckle, forgetting my shame.
My homework's a tale of adventure and fun,
But the clock's ticking down; I'm on the run!

They offer me snacks that will spark my delight,
Brownies from Jupiter, what a strange bite!
While planets remind me that I have to write,
My daydreams are wild, taking off at night.

In laughter and chaos, the galaxies spin,
As I find the resilience buried within.
With every new journey, my worries take flight,
I'll tackle my homework, just not tonight!

Whispers of the Wormhole

Through the wormhole I peek, what a sight to behold,
Homework's forgotten, that's just how it's rolled.
The aliens giggle, they dance in a trance,
While I trip over questions and miss every chance.

They invite me on board for a quick little chat,
Trading my essays for intergalactic spat.
"Who needs equations when we can play games?"
While I try to recall all my teacher's claims.

I share my frustration with a sigh and a grin,
Their laughter erupts as they spin me in spin.
My science report's crumpled, oh what a disgrace,
Yet here in this journey, I'm finding my place.

The starry confusion ignites every thought,
In this cosmic riddle, some lessons were taught.
While deadlines approach, I'll smile through the whip,
For laughter and learning are part of the trip!

Celestial Crayons and Cosmic Creativity

With crayons of starlight, I draw the unknown,
Galaxies swirling in shades I have grown.
My homework's a canvas where ideas can flow,
Creative explosions in a cosmic show.

Elves from the nebulae join in the fun,
Crafting equations while we splash some sun.
Our pencils are rocket ships zooming with glee,
As I scribble my dreams in this wild jubilee.

But reality calls with its deadlines and tests,
Yet here, every failure's a thrilling quest.
So I package my drawings in the light of the moon,
To turn in tomorrow, and hum a bright tune.

In realms of imagination, the homework's a breeze,
With laughter and colors, there's nothing to freeze.
So here's to the cosmos, with crayons in hand,
Creativity soars in this vast, wondrous land!

Homework Left in Zero Gravity

My math notes drifted away,
Floating like stars in the fray.
I chased them high, my pen in hand,
But zero gravity had other plans.

The science project took flight too,
Zooming past the neighbor's view.
I swear it winked, then spun around,
Kids giggled hard, laughter abound.

In this cosmic classroom craze,
Lost in space for many days.
My homework's now a starry sight,
Wish me luck for tomorrow's night.

So if you see my schoolwork roam,
Tell it to find its way back home.
I'll keep my feet on solid ground,
While homework dances all around!

The Curious Case of Missing Pages

Pages missing from my stack,
One minute there, the next, whack!
I accused my dog, he just played,
But sneaky aliens might invade.

A flip and flop, where did they go?
The last one showed a monstrous glow.
Math and science might make a show,
They'd laugh at my grades if they'd know!

I'll search the fridge and under beds,
They must be hiding somewhere, I said.
In the backyard, a strange sight,
Kites made of paper, caught in flight!

If only the intergalactic zoo,
Had a section for lost pages too.
I'll bring my friends and set up camp,
To find my work with a funny stamp!

Space Invaders and Study Guides

Invaders landed on my desk,
Turning study time grotesque.
They stole my guides and laughed out loud,
"Who needs homework? We're so proud!"

With laser beams they zapped my notes,
While I was stuck in my own quotes.
"Write some more!" they yelled in glee,
While I just wanted to be free!

I gave a shout, "Can you return,
The things you took? It's my big turn!"
They scratched their heads, with eyes so wide,
Then in a flash, they went to hide.

Now, with comics and candy wrappers,
My study guides? Just funny clappers!
They say and cheer, "We'll come again!"
To steal your work, just for the fun then!

Probing My Study Schedule

In the middle of my study spree,
Came strange sounds, oh, what could it be?
With probes and gadgets, they took a look,
My study schedule? An open book!

They scribbled notes with care and flair,
While I just stared, caught unaware.
"What's this?" they asked, "Boring routine?"
"I need it back!" I gave a keen scream.

They laughed and danced around my chair,
"Let's make it fun, don't you despair!"
They drew up plans for a galactic cram,
With snacks and games, an interstellar jam!

So now my studying is a blast,
With probes and fun that haul and cast.
Homework's cool when visitors land,
Just don't forget a helping hand!

The Homework Hitch at Midnight

In the still of night, my books took flight,
Chased by little green guys with eyes so bright.
They flipped through pages, laughed with glee,
Declaring, "Math is tough, but it's fun for we!"

My equations danced, and my essays sang,
As space critters jived, and the darkness rang.
They turned my notes into an outer space show,
I laughed and wondered, "Where will this go?"

With a final flourish, they zipped away,
Leaving my homework in disarray.
I sighed and smiled at this wild delight,
Perhaps my books will come back tonight!

So if your work goes missing, don't despair,
It may be out there with others to share.
Just look to the stars, and you may find,
Homework in space, left freely behind!

Disco on Saturn: A Homework Adventure

Under Saturn's rings, a disco ball shone,
While homework assignments danced on their own.
Math problems boogied with a funky beat,
History notes shimmied on colorful feet.

A textbook twist caught me by surprise,
As science facts swirled before my eyes.
"Join the party!" a comet called out,
I grabbed my pencil, swirling roundabout.

Gyrating graphs in a rhythm divine,
Spelling bees buzzing to a cosmic line.
I lost all track of my due dates and time,
In a swirling galaxy, everything's fine!

But as the music faded, I found my way,
Back to my desk, the bills to pay.
A note from Saturn? "Next time you're near,
Bring some snacks for us, and have no fear!"

Intergalactic Inquiry and Academic Alienation

I typed my questions into the vast unknown,
Waiting for answers in the galaxy's phone.
Instead of wisdom, what did I see?
A friendly Martian offering tea!

"Homework's a bore, let's play some games!"
He taught me calculus without any names.
With a zap and a zoom, my fears disappeared,
As we solved for X and laughed without fear.

His probing eyes sparkled with mischief grand,
I forgot my worries, oh ain't this just grand?
We flew through the cosmos on paper planes,
Leaving behind all our pesky refrains.

But when the bell rang, I flew back to earth,
With stars in my eyes and a new sense of mirth.
An intergalactic friend I now hold dear,
Maybe my homework will never reappear!

Assignments from the Asteroid Belt

Through the asteroid belt, my homework did roam,
On a rocket of paper, it found a new home.
Spelling tests floated like comets on high,
While science projects whizzed past my eye.

A rock named Rocky called out, "What's the plan?"
He doodled in craters, building a span.
"Let's teach these asteroids to write and to rhyme,
We'll start a new school, and have fun every time!"

Assignments galore, in a cosmic parade,
Each asteroid danced, as they cunningly played.
With no reason to fret, I joined in their spree,
My homework's adventures were wild and carefree.

But soon it was time to return to my room,
With thoughts of the asteroids clear in the gloom.
And though it was chaos, I'd do it again,
Homework in space? Oh, what a mad pen!

UFOs and Unfinished Essays

In the night, they zoomed bright,
Taking papers, what a sight!
My essay's gone, oh what a blunder,
Zooming ships made me wonder.

Chasing thoughts in the cool night,
Scrambled notes take off in flight.
High above with no care shown,
My deadline's lost, I groan alone.

They want math or maybe art,
I scribbled fast, but not the heart.
Instead, they took my jumbled dream,
Left me howling, it seems obscene!

Next time, I'll lock my door tight,
No homework left in plain sight.
Though they dance among the stars,
I'll keep my work safe from their cars!

Cosmic Conundrums of Conscience

A creature asked, "What's this paper?"
I replied, "It's nothing greater."
With tentacles, it scratched its head,
"Can we use it instead of bread?"

In a school where math gets tough,
I found strange aliens quite rough.
They offered stars for a few notes,
But I still wanted those wild quotes!

"Can't share my work!" I firmly said,
As they eyed my homework with dread.
Try as they might to trade for snacks,
I clutched my paper, "No time for hacks!"

With such cosmic twists of fate,
Homework woes cascade like fate.
For every paper, lesson learned,
Stellar friends need help—adjourned!

Descendants of the Distant Galaxy

A ship appeared in a flash so bright,
With beings giggling, such a weird sight.
"Your homework's taken, don't you see?"
They danced around, sipping tea!

One offered chips, another a pen,
In exchange for essays, "When can we begin?"
I laughed at their curious little ways,
Trading for snacks in cosmic plays.

Oh, distant cousins from beyond the stars,
Bringing laughter from Mars to the bars.
With homework gone, I shrugged my plight,
Sharing a snack seemed just right!

They scribbled on my sheets with glee,
My flowery words, not meant to be.
Cosmic heirs with shining eyes,
Making school fun, oh what a surprise!

Stellar Scribbles and Lost Lines

In the yard, paper flew like a kite,
Scribbles swirling in the moonlight.
They laughed as my letters took to the sky,
Chasing after, oh how they'd fly!

"Is this language? Or is it art?"
One asked with a very weird start.
"Just notes for class, not a grand feat,"
But they thought it was a cosmic treat!

With each line written, I lost my mind,
They took the punchlines, that's unkind!
"Come back, please!" I begged in vain,
While they scribbled in my brain.

As stars twinkled, bright and clear,
My homework transformed to cosmic cheer.
With lost lines and laughter in tow,
Who knew school could shine like a show?

Beings from Beyond and Bizarre Breakdowns

In the night sky, ships zoom and glide,
They snatch my papers, oh what a ride!
With antennas twitching, they laugh and tease,
While I search for notes, down on my knees.

They doodle on math, they scribble on art,
Leaving me puzzled, oh where to start!
Giggles erupt from their curious crew,
As my science fair project turns rainbow hue.

They ask for grammar tips, what a delight!
While I chase them around in a comic fright.
What should I tell them? "You're doing it wrong!"
But they just chuckle and hum a strange song.

With a wink and a wave, they zoom out of sight,
Leaving chaos in class, oh what a night!
I'll laugh with my friends about this wild spree,
If only my teacher would just let it be.

Homework and the Great Galactic Grievance

My math sheet vanished, a cosmic joke,
The aliens snatched it, oh what a poke!
They traded it for shiny things from space,
But I just want grades, can't keep up the pace!

They scribbled on history—what a sight!
Giant robots fought through the day and night.
Oh, who knew Julius Caesar was so sly?
While sipping tea with a pigeon from the sky?

I brought my report to the interstellar store,
But all I got back were strange cookies galore.
"Delicious," they said, "but what's your excuse?"
I shrugged with a grin, "My homework's in use!"

While I ponder this mess, snacks fill my hand,
I'll ace this quiz, that's the master plan!
Maybe someday they'll return what they took,
And I'll get an A for my alien book!

Abduction and Absenteeism in Academia

A bright light flashed, my study disrupted,
An alien came, my world interrupted.
"Come with me, let's solve this riddle,"
My homework disintegrated like soft little twiddle.

They whisked me away, oh what a spree,
Through galaxies where science is free.
But how can I learn when I'm lost in the void?
This cosmic adventure is getting annoying!

With probes and beams, they take notes galore,
"Can we borrow this?" Oh, what a chore!
"Sure, just be gentle with my trusty old pen!"
They nod with delight and zap me back when.

To my desk I return with stories to tell,
But my math test is looming—oh, what the hell!
I'll write 'extraterrestrial' on the first line,
They might just understand, especially in 9!

Studies on the Edge of Reality

My textbook's floating near the ceiling light,
An alien student just took flight!
With laughter they whirl, a bizarre sight,
In cosmic classrooms, everything's bright.

They jotted down formulas with three extra Z's,
And turned lunch into color-spouting freeze.
"Can we have recess for just one more hour?"
I nod with a grin, their energy's a power!

They claim they know math, but can't quite divide,
I help them with fractions, swell with pride.
"We're all from the cosmos, no need to compete,"
Little did I know they'd turn in my sheet!

With galaxies spinning in laughter and cheer,
I realize my studies just spread far and near.
So let's make a pact, homework can wait,
Together we'll learn, it's never too late!

Homework Under a Nebula

Late at night, my work was due,
But a cloud of stars sang loudly too.
With pens and paper, I made a fight,
Yet the cosmos giggled and stole the light.

Each math equation caught in a breeze,
Danced and twirled like floating leaves.
My pencil vanished in the galactic game,
While laughter echoed, calling my name.

Space owls hooted at my lost sheet,
While comets rushed by, quick on their feet.
Time slipped away, my deadline in shambles,
As meteors paraded, with frolicsome gambles.

So here I sit, with a cheerful sigh,
Waving goodbye to the problems that fly.
Homework forgotten on a star-sparkled trip,
With cosmic giggles on my homework flip.

The Scribbles of Starlit Shenanigans

A paper spaceship zips through space,
With doodles of aliens all over the place.
Math problems bouncing in zero-grav,
While a quirky robot helps me to halve.

My paragraphs transform into flying fish,
Wishing for school to grant me a wish.
An art project glows in a violet hue,
Boredom ceases when stars come into view.

Sentient crayons rolling away,
Decide to star in a cosmic play.
Homework is lost, traded for fun,
As meteor showers start to run.

Chasing time in this stellar gig,
With wiggles and squiggles, I dance a jig.
The universe laughs, it's all in a whirl,
While I spin around, homework's a swirl.

Assignment Anomalies from Planet Z

From worlds unknown, they sent my task,
Written in glitter, a strange sort of flask.
Jumbled letters, a riddle wrapped tight,
Homework beamed in from a ship's spotlight.

The cover page glows with a vibrant hue,
While instructions dance, like they're new to you.
A creature there scribbles fishy designs,
Flipping my brain into wiggly lines.

"Read it backwards," they cheekily tease,
While my logic contorts, but I feel such ease.
Unanswered queries float in the air,
As I giggle madly, caught in their snare.

With laughter shared, we all convene,
The strangest assignment I've ever seen.
Homework from Z takes me on a trip,
With cosmic giggles, I let my mind skip.

Chronicles of Cosmic Conundrums

In a world where stars decide what's due,
I find my grades in a constellation zoo.
Papers pirouetting like shooting stars,
Tasks are misplaced amid laughter from Mars.

A quiz full of doodles takes flight so free,
As space critters join in studying with glee.
They squabble and squeak, all while I sit,
Got lost in their chatter, forgetting the bit.

The countdown begins, the pressure's a feat,
But giggles afloat keep my heart light on beat.
Cosmic creatures wave, their antics so grand,
Chasing my worries to some distant land.

So as comets drift past with colorful trails,
I toss my old worries like forgotten tales.
With laughter as fuel, I skip past the stress,
In this universe bright, I'll surely impress!

Cosmic Creatures and Cosmic Curiosity

In a galaxy far, far away,
Strange beings dance and play.
They juggle stars and twirl in space,
With a grin on their funny face.

They peek through Earth with big green eyes,
Curious about our silly lies.
One tried to eat a math test sheet,
Declared it was a tasty treat!

With laughter bouncing off the moon,
They claimed they'd return real soon.
To learn of fractions, they would dive,
In a cosmic quest for the best high five!

So when your homework starts to wane,
Remember, it's all just an alien game.
They might just be the reason why,
Your grades are low, so don't you cry!

Homework Rescued by UFOs

One afternoon, my work was lost,
My heart sank, I worried at the cost.
But whoosh! A saucer spun through the air,
My paper vanished without a care.

The doorbell rang, to my surprise,
A crew of beings with big blue eyes.
They waved my homework, what a sight!
Said they'd return it by night!

They scanned my essays, giggled loud,
Then took a selfie—proudly they bowed.
With a zap and a flash, it was clear,
My homework was safe, and I had no fear!

When they left, I felt quite grand,
Waving a pencil in alien hand.
So if you lose your study tools,
Just wait for UFOs—those trusty fools!

The Cosmic Classroom Crisis

In class one day, what a shock!
The board was covered with a rock.
My teacher gasped, what could it be?
A puzzling mystery for all to see.

From under the desk came a loud zap,
And out popped creatures dressed like a chap.
They claimed to teach from Nebula High,
I just sat there, wide-eyed, oh my!

Lessons on planets, math in disguise,
Geometry shaped like pies!
With purple chalk, they drew a star,
And turned the classroom into a bazaar.

So when your school day feels like a slog,
Remember those beings, not a fog.
They turned our crisis into a treat,
Making learning cosmic and so sweet!

Mysteries from Beyond the Milky Way

What's that noise outside my door?
A spaceship landed, oh what a score!
Creatures popped out with shiny tools,
And turned my yard into cosmic pools!

They peered at grass like it was gold,
And laughed at stories we'd been told.
They tried to make a sandwich, too,
With stardust bread and jelly-blue.

In every corner, they made a mess,
But their giggles, I must confess,
Made me wonder, as they took flight,
If homework's a plan, with galaxies bright.

So if you hear a ruckus one night,
Don't lock your door—hold your fears tight!
For from the stars, true friends may sway,
And laugh with you in a fun new way!

Interstellar Interruption

In the night, a bright flash,
Homework vanished in a dash.
Little green hands took my notes,
Now they're plotting intergalactic quotes.

Crammed in my bag, there's no room,
For visits from this cosmic zoo.
They scribble math in alien ink,
In a language that makes my brain shrink.

Their laughter echoes across the skies,
While I chase them with bewildered sighs.
When I said, 'You can borrow my pen,'
I didn't mean 'Come back now and then!'

So here I sit with a puzzled face,
While they dance through interstellar space.
Could they return with my missing sheets?
Or will I face my teacher's feasts?

Lost Letters from Lightyears Away

A postcard from Mars appeared last week,
It said, 'Earthlings, your papers are bleak!'
With doodles of spaceships and stars,
I pondered if they'd gone too far.

My essay on space was quite a sight,
They scribbled notes all day and night.
'Physics is weird,' quipped a Martian sage,
As I flipped through their interstellar page.

Returning my work, they sent back quips,
'Take better notes, or take more trips!'
With every curveball tossed my way,
I wondered if they'd ever want to stay.

As my grades curdled and wilted like cheese,
I laughed, 'Oh please, just give me some peace!'
Emails from Saturn, feedback from Venus,
What a way to learn, that's their genius!

Space-Time Studies Gone Awry

I planned a project on time travel,
But ended up in a cosmic gravel.
My timeline jumbled, a wiggly line,
I forgot where I put my cereal swine.

Instead of formulas, I drew doodles,
In my sketchbook of whirling poodles.
The wormhole closed right in my face,
Leaving me lost in this bizarre place.

A note from the future said, 'Good luck!'
While I tried to decipher a marshy muck.
Perhaps I'd done a teensy mistake,
Like mixing up physics with a cupcake bake.

Now I'm stuck between here and there,
While my classmates giggle, thinking it fair.
So if you find my lost time thesis,
Just send it back, I'd love some peace!

Universe Unplugged: The Missing Assignment

My homework fell through a cosmic door,
Into a dimension I can't explore.
With planets spinning and stars in spree,
I can only wonder where it might be.

I tried to plug in my thoughts anew,
But my Wi-Fi vanished—true, it's true!
As comets raced past my blinking screen,
I hesitated to create a scene.

Messages floated from worlds unbound,
With pictures of my name, lost and found.
'Stop by our galaxy, it's quite a blast!'
I sighed, 'Sure, but I need my grades fast!'

So here I stand in a cosmic fright,
Dreaming of essays lost in the night.
With giggles from galaxies, I must confess,
This school project just became a mess!

www.ingramcontent.com/pod-product-compliance
Lightning Source LLC
Chambersburg PA
CBHW070748220426
43209CB00083B/115